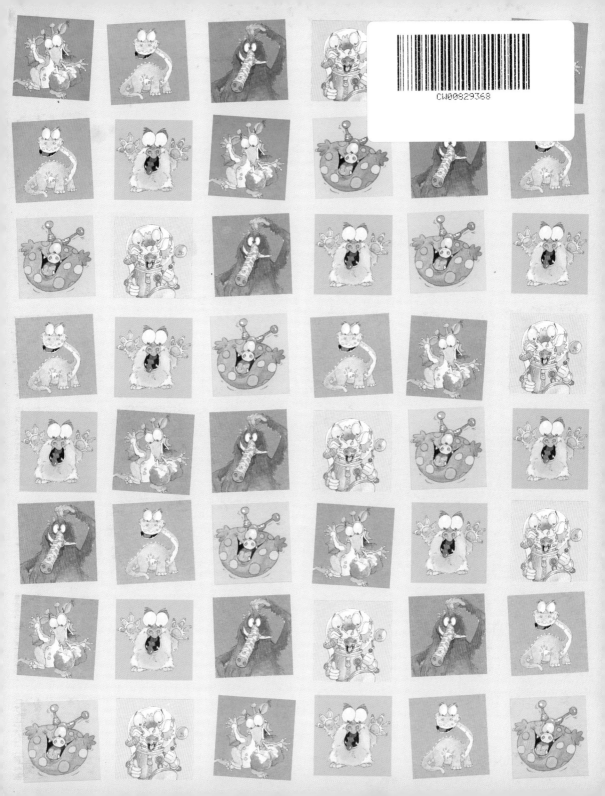

This book belongs to

....

Five-minute
MONSTER
— Tales —

p

CONTENTS

Sparky and the
BABY DRAGON

8

BOINK

14

NESSY
of the lake

20

SNIFFLE

26

The Fluff
MONSTERS

32

Wibble and the
EARTHLINGS

38

Sparky and the
BABY DRAGON

S parky was a young dragon who lived in a cave far, far away. Now, as you know, dragons can breathe flames out of their noses! But you may not know that baby dragons have to *learn* how to do it.

"Watch me," said Mum to Sparky, and she puffed out a long flame and lit a candle.

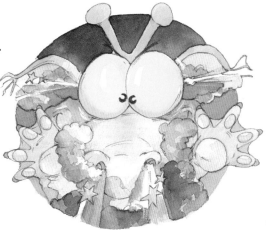

"Now watch me," said Dad, and he breathed over some logs in the fireplace and made a fire. Sparky watched very carefully.

"Now watch *me*," he said, and he puffed until he was purple in the face. Two or three little sparks came out of his nose and ears!

"Bravo!" said Dad.

"It's coming on!" said Mum.

Sparky felt very proud.

One day Mum and Dad had to go out.

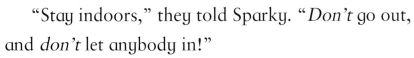

"Stay indoors," they told Sparky. "*Don't* go out, and *don't* let anybody in!"

"Why?" asked Sparky.

"Because of the wicked witch," said Mum. "She hates little dragons and turns them into teapots, just for fun!"

"Oh!" said Sparky. But he didn't mind staying in. He had some new toy knight figures to play with.

He had just started when he heard a bell outside.

"Ting-a-ling," it went, "ting-a-ling." And then a voice said, "Ice-cream! Ice-cream! Come and get your ice-cream!"

Sparky peeped out. Outside was a brightly painted ice-cream cart. Sitting behind the wheel was an old woman with a big grin.

"Come and get your ice cream, Sparky," said the woman, and she laughed!

It was a loud, cackling laugh. When Sparky heard it, he knew it was the witch. He slammed the door and locked it.

The witch pedalled off in a rage.

"Phew!" thought Sparky, as he settled down to his knights and dragons game. "That was close."

The afternoon passed peacefully.

Then, the doorbell rang. "Who is it?" Sparky called out.

"It's Uncle Jack," said a voice, "I've come to take you fishing."

Sparky liked Uncle Jack, and he liked fishing! He went to open the door. Then he stopped.

"Is it really you?" he asked.

"Of course it is," laughed Uncle Jack.

But, as soon as Sparky heard the loud, cackling

laugh, he knew it was the witch.

"Go away!" he shouted.
"Go away!"

Then he heard someone crying. He peered through the door and saw a baby dragon on the doorstep!

"I've lost my mummy!" sobbed the dragon.

"You'd better come in," said Sparky. He opened the door! The baby dragon rushed in! Then …

"Got you!" snapped the baby dragon. And turned into the witch!

Sparky gasped.

The witch raised her wand and shouted the magic word "Ta-ra-ra-boom-de-ay!" and started to spin very fast.

Sparky closed his eyes and puffed as hard as he could. When he opened them he had a big surprise!

The witch was surrounded by a puff of smoke.

Sparky watched in amazement as smoke cleared. Then, would you believe it, *she had turned herself into a bright, blue teapot!*

Just then Mum and Dad came back.

"Have you had any trouble while we've been away?" asked Mum, kissing him.

"Not much!" said Sparky. "But, next time you go out, can I come with you?"

"Of course you can!" said Mum. "Now why don't I make some tea in this nice new teapot!"

BoINK

Boink was a small round monster. His name was Boink, but it was also the sound he made when he moved around. You and I can walk and run, but Boink the monster bounced like a ball – BOINK! BOINK! BOINK! – until he got where he was going. He looked like a space-hopper toy and he was rubbery too, to help him bounce.

Boink lived happily in an empty dog kennel at the bottom of Joe's garden. No one knew he was there. He couldn't even remember how he had got there, but that didn't worry him. Boink didn't worry about anything. He was a happy little monster and he enjoyed life. There was just one problem – he didn't have anything to play with.

Boink often watched Joe playing. Joe didn't have anyone to play with but he had lots of toys. Boink watched him as he took all his cars out of a big green box. He watched as he lined up all the red cars together, then all the blue cars, and then all the yellow cars. He watched as he moved the cars around. When Joe did this he made a strange sound.

"Brmmm! Brmmm!" he went, "Brmmm! Brmmm! Brmmm!"

Boink practised making the noise at night when no one was listening.

"Brmmm!" he said softly, and then louder, "Brmmm! Brmmm!" But it wasn't any fun without the cars. Boink wanted some toys of his own. So he decided to borrow some!

One night, when Joe was asleep, Boink bounced in through an open window. In Joe's bedroom there were toys everywhere. There were aeroplanes on a shelf and a train set on the floor. Boink took two cars out of the green box. Then he bounced out of the window and back to the dog kennel.

The first thing Joe
noticed the next
morning was that
some of his cars
were missing.

"Mum," he
called, "have you seen
my cars?"

But Joe's mum hadn't seen
them. The next day Joe whizzed around the garden
with his aeroplanes going, "Neeaw! Neeaw!"

Boink watched Joe playing, and that night he
took two aeroplanes from Joe's bedroom!

"Mum," said Joe, going into the kitchen, "my
aeroplanes are missing!"

"Did you leave them in the garden?" asked Mum.
But Joe knew he hadn't. Joe had to play with his
train set instead.

That night Joe only pretended to go to sleep. He
couldn't believe his eyes! He saw a roly-poly monster

bounce in through the window
and take his train set! As
Boink bounced back out of
the window Joe leapt out
of bed and watched him
disappear with the train set
into the old kennel.

The next day, after
breakfast, Joe went straight
to the dog kennel and peeped
inside. There, fast asleep, was a roly-poly monster.
And all around him were Joe's missing toys! Joe was
so surprised, he gave a startled yelp. Boink woke up.

"Brmmm! Brmmm!" said Boink grinning.

"What do you mean, Brmmm! Brmmm!?" said Joe.

"Neeaw! Neeaw!" said Boink.

"You only say Brmmm! Brmmm! when you're
playing with cars," said Joe. "And you only say
Neeaw! Neeaw! when you're playing aeroplanes."

"Neeaw! Neeaw!" said Boink.

"You can play with me if you like," said Joe, "but you must promise never to take my toys without asking."

"Chuff! Chuff!" said Boink.

"Right then, let's join up all the railway lines so that we can play with the train set," said Joe.

"Toot! Toot!" said Boink.

And that's what they did. When they had finished, the train set went in and out of the kennel and the engine went round and round.

When Joe's mum looked out of the window, she was pleased to see that Joe had found his missing toys. And she was surprised to see a space-hopper in the garden!

NESSY
of the Lake

Nessy was a very shy monster. She was also very big. She was so big she could fill a swimming pool! Luckily, she lived in a large, deep lake, so no one ever saw her.

Nessy was too shy to go out and make friends. She once tried making friends with a small fish, but the fish bit her nose and swam away! Nessy shrugged. She was fed up. She hoped she'd find a friend soon.

One lovely sunny day Nessy peeped above the surface and saw a small boy fishing with his grandpa on the bank. The boy had a rod and a net and a shiny, red bucket.

He fished all day but didn't catch anything.

The next day Nessy watched again.

The little boy still didn't catch any fish.

"Watch out for ripples on the surface of the lake, Billy," said his grandpa. "Ripples mean fish!" Then Billy's grandpa nodded off to sleep.

Billy watched the surface of the lake for signs of ripples. Nessy watched Billy. All was quiet and still.

Then Nessy decided to go a bit closer … and closer … and closer still.

Billy stared at the ripples on the lake. He watched them coming closer … and closer … and closer still.

"Boo!" said Nessy suddenly splashing her head out of the water.

"Wow!" said Billy, staring. "You're not a fish – you're a monster!"

Nessy tried a friendly smile, showing all her teeth.

"Are you going to eat me?" asked Billy, alarmed.

"Of course not," said Nessy. "I want to be friends."

"You've got lots of big teeth," said Billy.

"Have I?" said Nessy. "Do they frighten you?"

"Not when you smile," said Billy.

Nessy smiled even wider.

"My name's Billy," said Billy. "What's yours?"

"Nessy," said Nessy. "What are you doing?" she asked Billy.

"I'm trying to catch a fish, but I'm not having much luck."

"I'll help," said Nessy. "Leave it to me!" and she started swimming very fast into the middle of the lake.

Then she disappeared! Billy stared at the middle of the lake. He stared for ages. Then the next thing he heard was Grandpa's voice saying, "Wake up, Billy!"

"I am awake," said Billy. "You'll never guess who I've been talking to, Grandpa!"

"Let me see," said Grandpa, "Old Mother Hubbard?"

"No," said Billy, "of course not."

"The Three Bears?"

"Grandpa!"

"Who then?"

"Nessy, of course, the monster who lives in the lake!"

"You've been dreaming, Billy!" smiled Grandpa.

"No I haven't," said Billy. "She came really close. And she splashed me, although she didn't mean to. Look … my shoes are all wet!" Grandpa looked.

"And she said she'd help me catch a fish," Billy went on.

"Well, it's time to go now,

Billy!" said Grandpa. "Don't forget your bucket!"

Billy picked up his bucket.

"Grandpa!" he said. "Look!"

Grandpa looked. There in Billy's bucket was the prettiest blue and gold fish he had ever seen.

"Well, I'll be blowed," said Grandpa.

Billy just grinned. Gently, he tipped the fish back into the water. Then he called out loudly, "See you, Nessy! See you tomorrow!"

And from the middle of the lake a big, shy monster waved back.

SNIFFLE

A long way away, in a jungle no one had ever been to before, lived the Sniffle monster. The famous explorer, Major Jolly, went into the jungle looking for new animals. First, he found a big, bright bird that strutted about showing everyone what a great tail it had. Then he found a new type of monkey that could knit socks! His greatest discovery, though, was when he came upon the MONSTER, in a tree, eating a banana.

Major Jolly got very excited! The monster was
intelligent! That means it could think like you and
me. Major Jolly knew it was intelligent because only
intelligent people eat bananas. Don't you think so?
Well Major Jolly did, because he liked bananas too.

The monster was quite ugly, but then he would
be, wouldn't he. He was big, ugly and covered in red
fur. His fingertips could touch the floor when he was
standing on the table!

Major Jolly decided to take him home to show his
wife. They flew back in a big
plane and the monster
sat on three seats
as well as a
passenger. The
famous
explorer's wife
met them at the
airport.

"This is the monster I discovered, Maud," said Major Jolly. "He doesn't speak English."

"How do you do?" Maud held out her hand.

"Howdeedoodee," repeated the monster. He took the lady's hand and sniffed it, and then danced her round the room in circles.

"I'll soon have him speaking English," said Maud, as they danced past for the third time.

Back home the monster wanted to dance with everyone at first! But just a few weeks later he began to look ill and sad. He coughed and sniffed and spluttered. His coat turned dull, and patches of fur fell out. And he had something really nasty running out of his nose. He spent all day trying to lie on the sofa without falling off.

When Maud visited, he wouldn't dance round the room with her. "My dear Monster," she said, "what's wrong with you?"

The monster had learned to speak by now.

"I am Sniffle monster!" he said. "I was taken away from jungle without friend. I must have this friend with me always, or I get ill! Stuff comes out of my nose! My friend is Hanky monster."

Maud thought she understood.

"And you need this Hanky monster ... umm... to wipe your nose for you?"

"No, no, no!" said Sniffle. "Hanky is a magician. He will make Sniffle dance again! Only Hanky monster knows secret magic potion."

Major Jolly was really sorry that he had taken the
Sniffle monster away from his Hanky monster. They
must go back to the jungle straight away, find the
Hanky monster, and Sniffle would be well again.
Just a few days later, they found the place in the
jungle where Major Jolly had camped before.
Suddenly, something that looked like a giant cabbage
hurtled through the bushes and threw itself at Sniffle.
Sniffle gave a whoop of joy! The cabbage and Sniffle
danced round the clearing until Sniffle was too tired
to move. The cabbage was the Hanky monster, of
course! It rushed back into the jungle.

"Gone to get magic potion," whispered Sniffle
weakly.

The Hanky monster came back with a drink in a coconut shell. Sniffle drank it and went straight to bed. Next morning his coat was shiny and his nose had stopped running. He danced with everyone.

The secret potion was amazing! Sniffle was well again. Major Jolly was desperate to know the secret of the magic drink.

"It's a secret!" was all the Hanky monster would say. But when Major Jolly got home there was a letter for him with SECRET MAGIC POTION – DON'T TELL ANY PEOPLE! written on the outside. He opened the letter eagerly. A photograph of Sniffle and Hanky fell out. The letter read …

HOT LEMON AND HONEY!

– The Fluff –
MONSTERS

This is the story of the Fluff monsters. Everyone has seen fluff under the bed. That's because the Fluff monsters live under beds. They need beds that are not too clean underneath.

The Fluff monsters only come out when it's dark. They don't know what the world outside beds is like in daylight. They think it's scary just being out during the day. Who knows what might be out in the daylight? Once, Fluff-boy was having a quiet

meal eating fluff and custard, when suddenly *the-magic-sucking-thing* appeared. It made a terrible noise as it came closer and closer. Then a tube with a brush on the end sucked up all the fluff under the bed after he'd spent ages collecting it!

But Fluff-boy had only ever lived under his bed. He wanted to know what it was like under other beds.

"Only naughty Fluff monsters go out in daylight," said Fluff-mummy, "and do you know what happens to naughty Fluff monsters?"

"No, I don't," said Fluff-boy, alarmed. "What?"

His mother put on a scary voice and said, *"The Little Girl will get you!"*

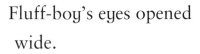

Fluff-boy's eyes opened wide.

"Who's the Little Girl?" he asked.

"The Little Girl is a monster who lives *in the bed!*" said Fluff-mummy. "She is really clean and pretty! She will take you away and wash you and put you in a room with sun shining through the windows! She will open the doors and fill the room with fresh air from *outside!*"

"That's horrible! I don't believe you," said Fluff-boy. "You're making it up!"

"Well, you'll just have to be good," said Fluff-mummy, "or you'll find out!"

"Well, I'm not scared of the Little Girl!" said Fluff-boy.

Fluff-boy wasn't going to be put off. He wanted

to know what it was like under other beds. One day, while everyone was asleep, Fluff-boy slipped away. Outside, bright sunlight filled the room.

"That must be the window Fluff-mummy told me about," thought Fluff-boy.

He wandered into the next room and found another bed to slide under. There were spiders and daddy-long-legs, cobwebs and lots and lots of fluff! It was perfect! So Fluff-boy ate some fluff (though he did miss his mum's home-made custard) and settled into his new home.

But Fluff-boy couldn't sleep, as he was thinking about the Little Girl. He had to see if she was real or not. Plucking up courage he poked his head out from under the bed. Carefully, he climbed up the bed covers until he could scramble over the top.

Suddenly, the Little Girl woke and sat up. Fluff-boy was so surprised he jumped with fright.

"Aaargh!" shrieked Fluff-boy.

"Aaargh!" screamed the Little Girl.

They scrambled to each end of the bed and stared at each other.

"You gave me a fright!" said Fluff-boy.

"*Me* frighten *you*?" said the Little Girl. "*You* frightened *me!*"

"Did I?" said Fluff-boy. "Why?"

"Well, you're the Bogeyman aren't you?" said the Little Girl.

"There's no such thing as the Bogeyman,"

laughed Fluff-boy. "I'm Fluff-boy. I've just moved in under this bed. Do you live in this bed too?"

"No, silly," said the Little Girl. "I just sleep here at night. I thought scary Bogeymen lived under the bed. But you're not scary at all!"

"How about this then?" asked Fluff-boy. He stuck his thumbs in his ears, wiggled his fingers and poked his tongue out. The Little Girl laughed.

"That's not at all scary!" she said. "*This* is scary," and she pulled the corners of her mouth out with her fingers and crossed her eyes.

And that was how Fluff-boy and the Little Girl discovered that there is nothing scary
under the bed or in it!

Wibble and the
EARTHLINGS

Wibble was from the planet Xog. He was on a mission. He'd been sent secretly to Earth to find out about Earthlings.

Wibble's spaceship wobbled on landing, but there wasn't too much damage. He radioed back to Xog to tell them his camera was broken.

"Just tell us what the Earthlings look like," said Captain Pimples, the leader of the Xogs, "and I'll draw them. Over!"

"I will," said Wibble. "Over and out!" He climbed down from the spaceship and looked around. There was a big sign saying ZOO.

"I wonder what that means," thought Wibble.

Wibble wobbled over to the nearest building and opened the door. He went up to a big wooden fence and saw his first Earthling. With its long neck, it leaned over the fence and gave Wibble a huge lick.

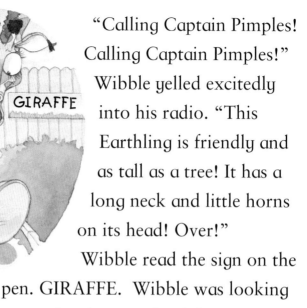

GIRAFFE

"Calling Captain Pimples! Calling Captain Pimples!" Wibble yelled excitedly into his radio. "This Earthling is friendly and as tall as a tree! It has a long neck and little horns on its head! Over!"

Wibble read the sign on the pen. GIRAFFE. Wibble was looking at a giraffe, of course, but because he didn't understand the signs, Wibble thought it must be an Earthling. Captain Pimples drew an Earthling with a long neck and two horns.

"Sounds okay so far!" said the Captain. "Tell me more. Over!"

Wibble wandered to the next fence, marked
ELEPHANT. He switched on the radio.

"It's an enormous Earthling! It has huge ears and
a long spout on the front like a teapot! Over!"

Captain Pimples quickly added the big ears and
the spout to his drawing.

Next, Wibble went into a building marked
AQUARIUM. He gazed around at the water tanks.

One had a sign that said: SQUID. "This Earthling has two huge eyes and is covered in orange spots! Over!" Wibble said into his radio. Captain Pimples added two huge eyes and orange spots to the drawing.

"Okay!" said Captain Pimples. "We've heard enough. Earthlings are big, hairy, have enormous

ears and a spout, two huge eyes and orange spots. A bit like us really! Over and out!"

So Captain Pimples led an expedition to Earth. That is when Mr Brown the zoo-keeper walked by. Mr Brown had quite a shock seeing them, but not half as much as the Xogs had seeing him.

"Aargh!" cried the Xogs, and ran back to their spaceship. They took off and didn't stop until they reached planet Xog. Captain Pimples found Earth on his map, crossed it off and wrote underneath, "BEWARE – MONSTERS!"

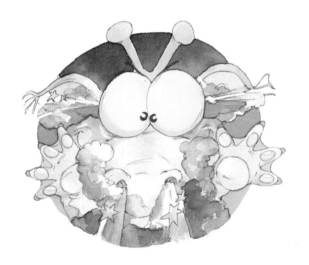

Written by Jan and Tony Payne, Likely Stories
Illustrated by Peter Rutherford
Language consultant: Betty Root
Design by Design Principals

This is a Parragon Book
First published in 2002

Parragon
Queen Street House
4 Queen Street
Bath BA1 1HE, UK

Printed in Spain

ISBN 0-75258-592-4

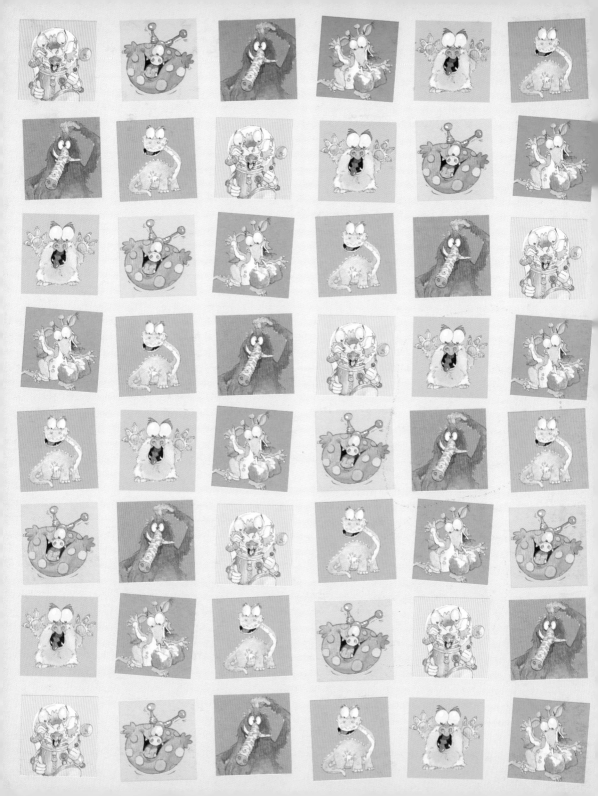